· THE OFFICIAL ·

LIARS'

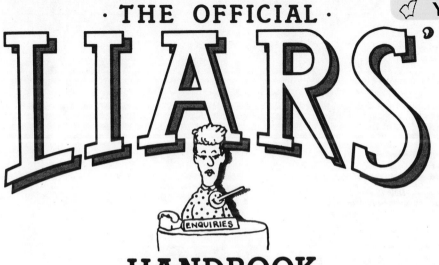

ENQUIRIES

HANDBOOK

· DAVID DALE ·

Illuminations by Matthew Martin

A Perigee Book

Perigee Books
are published by
The Putnam Publishing Group
200 Madison Avenue
New York, NY 10016

Published simultaneously in Canada by
General Publishing Co. Limited, Toronto

Library of Congress Cataloging-in-Publication Data
Dale, David, date.
* The official liars' handbook.*

* "A Perigee book."*
* 1. Truthfulness and falsehood—Anecdotes, facetiae,*
satire, etc. I. Title.
PN6231.T74D35   1987   818'.5402   87-10755
ISBN 0-399-51398-1

First published in Australia
by Angus & Robertson Publishers in 1986
First published in the United Kingdom
by Angus & Robertson (UK) Ltd in 1986

Printed in the United States of America
1 2 3 4 5 6 7 8 9 10

Contents

Introduction v

Advertising Agencies 1

Babies 2

The Building Trade 4

Car Repair 6

Childbirth 7

Computers 8

Delicatessens 10

Diets 11

Drivers 12

Hairdressing 13

Home Dressmaking 14

Home Handymen 15

International Travel 17

Journalism 20

Kids 22

The Law 23

Local Government **26**

Love 28

Meetings 30

Men 31

Model Making 33

Nursing 34

Officials 35

Parents 36

Parties 37

The Personnel Office 39

Political Press Secretaries 40

Publishing 42

Radio Interviewing 44

Restaurants 45

Sales Assistants 47

Teachers 49

The Theater 51

Train Travel 53

Universities 54

Your 30th Birthday 56

Acknowledgements 57

Introduction

This book will change your life. Two million copies already in print. Soon to be a major motion picture. If any of those statements seem the slightest bit plausible to you, you need our help. You are not yet skeptical enough to survive to the end of the 20th century. Didn't you realise you are living in the age of The Big Lie?

Just think how the number of synonyms for untruthfulness keeps increasing . . . mendacity, misspeaking, fibbing, prevarication, embroidering the truth, deception, evasiveness, distortion, fabrication, terminological inexactitude. It was that pioneer in modern mendacity, Richard "I am not a crook" Nixon, who was responsible for the greatest post-war verbal breakthrough in the field. Under challenge from the press as the Watergate evidence contradicted what the president had said, Nixon's press secretary, Ronald L. Ziegler, declared: "This is the operative statement. The others are inoperative."

But it's not only politicians who are at it these days. Every field of human endeavor, whether work or play, has accumulated its own set of lies. And that's what this book is about. We've catalogued them, so that gullible people like you can be prepared wherever you go. This is your survival manual. On these pages you'll find 450 of the Great Lies of the 20th century, handily divided into subject areas which, in turn, are presented in alphabetical order. Look up your own occupation . . . hairdresser, nurse, computer operator, civil servant (that's under "Great Lies of Officials"). How many of the lies did you use today? Look up your hobby . . . model making, home dressmaking, travel, eating out, making love. How many of the lies were you told today?

Now you can see why this book was such a wise purchase. Keep it with you at all times. Buy extra copies so your friends can be as well warned as you (or almost as well warned—don't forget to tear out the pages that cover YOUR lies). You'll never regret it. Trust us.

David Dale

Advertising Agencies

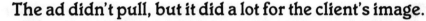

■ The ad didn't pull, but it did a lot for the client's image. ■ Our audience ratings are down, but we all know about surveys, don't we? ■ We're going to be late with the artwork, but wait until you see the treatment. ■ Sure Andy's a hopeless drunk, but he's a brilliant creative director. ■ They haven't taken over our agency — we've merged. ■ We didn't sack Andrew, he resigned. ■ This commercial cries out for atmosphere — we've got to shoot it in the Bahamas.

Babies

■ New babies sleep 18 hours a day. ■ You'll soon get into a routine. ■ She can't be hungry. ■ Soaking will remove even the stubbornest stains. ■ You can manage without a dryer. ■ He'll sleep through once he's weaned. ■ You can't spoil a baby. ■ You look well. ■ You can sleep when the baby sleeps. ■ Nobody will care if the house is untidy. ■ We'll take turns. ■ All babies do that. ■ Older siblings will enjoy helping. ■ He loves other kids. ■ She loves vegetables. ■ Of course he can get down the stairs by himself. ■ She doesn't usually cry this much. ■ I never hit him. ■ All you have to do is say no and she'll stop. ■ Just leave him to cry — he'll go to sleep eventually. ■ I had to get it dry cleaned anyway.

The Building Trade

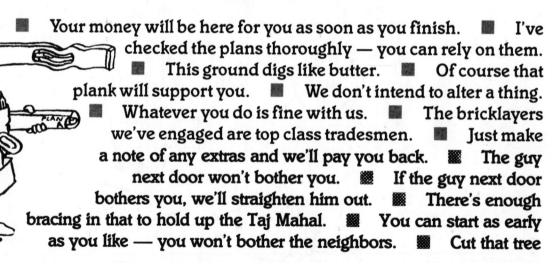

■ Your money will be here for you as soon as you finish. ■ I've checked the plans thoroughly — you can rely on them. ■ This ground digs like butter. ■ Of course that plank will support you. ■ We don't intend to alter a thing. ■ Whatever you do is fine with us. ■ The bricklayers we've engaged are top class tradesmen. ■ Just make a note of any extras and we'll pay you back. ■ The guy next door won't bother you. ■ If the guy next door bothers you, we'll straighten him out. ■ There's enough bracing in that to hold up the Taj Mahal. ■ You can start as early as you like — you won't bother the neighbors. ■ Cut that tree down if you like — there're no environmentalists in this area.  No way you could get bogged there. ■ We'll look back on this and laugh. ■ Keep backing up — there's plenty of room.

Car Repair

The quote covers everything. ■ It'll be ready this afternoon. ■ I'm waiting for a part. ■ Spares cost a fortune on these foreign jobs. ■ It's a slight knock in the tappets. ■ After this it'll go like a rocket. ■ It's a bit more complicated than we thought. ■ If I did that, it would only put off the problem. By paying more now you'll save a lot later. ■ The last person who worked on this must have been a gorilla. ■ These retreads are just as good as the new ones. I use them on my own car. ■ It'll be fine for the long trip. ■ Yeah, yeah, I can see the guy working on it now. ■ Of course it's guaranteed. ■ Those marks were there when you brought it in. ■ No, that's not covered by the warranty. ■ It will settle down after a bit of driving.

Childbirth

■ It doesn't hurt. ■ You forget all about it once the child is born. ■ The speculum won't be cold. ■ Your pelvis is quite a good size. ■ You have childbearing hips. ■ You won't need an episiotomy. ■ You can have an epidural whenever you want. ■ The anesthesiologist will be here in a minute. ■ Doctor's on his way. ■ You're doing really well. ■ This one will just pop out. ■ The worst's over now. ■ You haven't bled very much. ■ Just a small tear, dear, it'll only need a stitch or two. ■ Baby's a little bit blue. ■ You'll only need a few days' rest. ■ You'll be back in a bikini in six weeks. ■ You can't get pregnant while you're breast feeding.

Computers

■ An eight-year-old could use this. ■ Oh yes, it's compatible with everything. ■ All software is included. ■ That software will be available when your machine is delivered. ■ There is no need for air conditioning. ■ You won't need any special training. ■ That's not likely to occur. ■ The screen will come back soon. ■ There's no harm in trying it — nothing can go wrong. ■ It's never done that before. ■ The system will give a paper-less office. ■ The manual explains everything.
■ You don't need to know about programming. ■ If you have any problems, all you have to do is ring us. ■ The next model will be compatible with this one. ■ What you see on the screen is what you get on paper. ■ The latest version fixes all the bugs in the earlier one. ■ The price is going up

next week because of the devaluation. ■ Someone must have erased my program. ■ You'll never have any need for more memory/disc space than this. ■ How could anybody need that much disc space? ■ The new development that will fix that will be out next week/November/year. ■ They don't make those chips any more. ■ Plug it in and away you go. ■ If kids can use them, so can adults.

Delicatessens

■ Oh yes, it was fresh this morning. ■ This salami isn't hot. ■ This cheese only ripens two weeks after the expiration date. ▨ It's meant to be moldy. ▨ This is our most popular line. ▨ The price is higher because it's a better quality. ▨ This is a very mild/strong cheese. ▨ It's just on special for today. ▨ I'll get you some leaner ham/bacon/pastrami from the cool room. ■ The smoked fish has a fairly mild aroma. ■ I've wrapped it in several layers of plastic so it won't leak. ■ It's very easy to prepare.
■ If you order a month before Christmas, I'll keep a turkey/ham for you.
▨ Of course it's kosher.

Diets

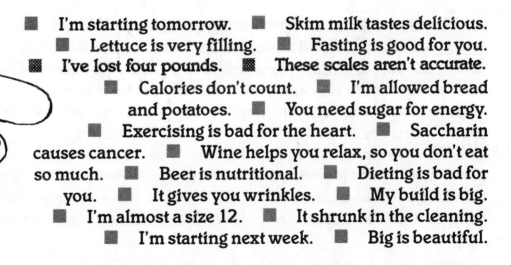

- I'm starting tomorrow.
- Skim milk tastes delicious.
- Lettuce is very filling.
- Fasting is good for you.
- I've lost four pounds.
- These scales aren't accurate.
- Calories don't count.
- I'm allowed bread and potatoes.
- You need sugar for energy.
- Exercising is bad for the heart.
- Saccharin causes cancer.
- Wine helps you relax, so you don't eat so much.
- Beer is nutritional.
- Dieting is bad for you.
- It gives you wrinkles.
- My build is big.
- I'm almost a size 12.
- It shrunk in the cleaning.
- I'm starting next week.
- Big is beautiful.

Drivers

I was just going the speed limit.   ▪   I only had the one.   ▪   The light was green when I started through the intersection.   ▪   What stop sign? ▪   Some sort of animal came from the bushes and caused me to swerve and I lost control.   ▪   He came from nowhere when I changed lanes.   ▪   I can steer perfectly well with one hand.   ▪   I was only drinking beer.   ▪   I never speed when I've been drinking.   ▪   You don't need to worry about your seat belt when you're only going half a mile.   ▪   I can walk without assistance.   ▪   My wife/husband normally drives.   ▪   I've been driving 40 years without an accident.   ▪   I only drink on weekends.   ▪   I was only going round the corner.   ▪   Never trust an elderly male driver with a hat on.

Hairdressing

■ I'm only taking off half an inch.   ■ I'll be with you in five minutes. ■ It's just the light in here.   ■ I use it myself.   ■ It's a new technique.   ■ The colour will fade.   ■ The perm will soften and drop.   ■ It will only take a day to get used to it.   ■ Lots of men have their hair lightened.   ■ It suits you.   ■ It's easy to manage. ■ You're not going bald.   ■ It's all the rage in New York.   ■ It looks better short.   ■ It won't be frizzy — just a soft curl.   ■ It's just dry scalp.   ■ I remember how I did it last time.   ■ It's very natural — no one would guess you've had streaks.   ■ I love cutting kids' hair.

Home Dressmaking

■   This pattern needs no adjustment/fits all figures/can be made in two hours/is easy for beginners.   ■   This machine sews through anything/over pins/perfect buttonholes/embroidery/overlock/ensures a professional result.   ■   This material will not fray/shrink/bleed/fade/need pattern matching/disappoint when made up/be beaten for value.   ■   This thread **never breaks/knots/needs color changing/sells cheaper elsewhere.**
■   That dress looks great/hangs evenly/fits like a dream/has identical sleeves/is not really puckered there/just needs a little pull here.

Home Handymen

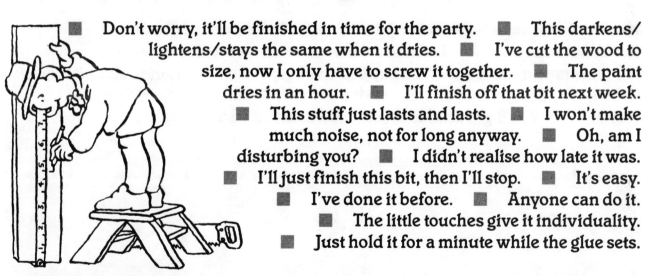

Don't worry, it'll be finished in time for the party. ■ This darkens/lightens/stays the same when it dries. ■ I've cut the wood to size, now I only have to screw it together. ■ The paint dries in an hour. ■ I'll finish off that bit next week. ■ This stuff just lasts and lasts. ■ I won't make much noise, not for long anyway. ■ Oh, am I disturbing you? ■ I didn't realise how late it was. ■ I'll just finish this bit, then I'll stop. ■ It's easy. ■ I've done it before. ■ Anyone can do it. ■ The little touches give it individuality. ■ Just hold it for a minute while the glue sets.

■ Municipal approval is not required. ■ No one will notice that. ■ It washes out. ■ I turned it off at the main tap/valve/switch. ■ This tape measure must be marked wrongly. ■ You don't need a licence to do a little thing like that. ■ Wait a second, I'll just smooth off that little bump. ■ You'll get used to it. ■ Of course it's strong enough.

International Travel

■ Don't buy it now, wait until the duty free at . . . ■ You don't need a visa for there. ■ There's no problem getting a visa at the border. ■ It's always nice in the autumn. ■ You don't have to get there early, it never leaves on time. ■ I'll be there to meet you. ■ The cyclone season is over. ■ All meals are included in the price. ■ Every room has a view of the sea. ■ It's only a minute from the beach. ■ The water is safe to drink. ■ I know someone who can give you a better exchange rate. ■ Give the porter all your bags — he won't say anything. ■ They don't weigh your luggage. ■ This is the cheapest shop in town. ■ The X-ray machine won't affect your film. ■ Room service will bring toilet paper immediately. ■ You don't have to check out till the next guests arrive.

■ There's no need to tip. ■ This appliance is guaranteed to work with your home electricity supply. ■ This appliance has an international guarantee. ■ The power failure will be over in a minute. ■ It's cheaper to take a taxi. ■ It doesn't rain much this time of year. ■ The rain will stop soon. ■ You'll have no problem finding someone who speaks English. ■ It will cool down later tonight. ■ Your taxi will come in a second. ■ The tour will be leaving any minute now. ■ There'll be no problem with customs. ■ The taxi driver will know where to take you.

Journalism

■ Of course I'll call back and read you the story. ■ There just wasn't enough space. ■ It's page one for sure. ■ Oh, I know it's your only photo of your husband and children — I'll definitely get it back to you tomorrow. ■ If you give this to me exclusively, I can promise you a good run. ■ Sorry to call you on a Sunday/so late/so early. ■ Of course I respect your right to privacy. ■ No, I'm not using a tape recorder. ■ That's not really my area. ■ It wasn't meant to imply you had AIDS. ■ She/he is expected back from lunch any minute now. ■ Yes, it is off the record. ■ Of course they won't sue. ■ I haven't had a chance to look at the press release yet. ■ I'll get him/her to phone you back. ■ I'll discuss it with the Bureau Chief/Copy Desk/Editor. ■ It is just for background. ■ That's interesting.

■ No, it wasn't intended to be a reference to you. ■ I'll check it out.
■ We'll put a correction in tomorrow. ■ I haven't had a drink all day/week/month/year/since I started. ■ That's not the way I wrote it.
■ I included that but rewrite cut it out. ■ Send a letter to the editor.
■ We can't run that for legal reasons. ■ I tried to contact you but your phone wasn't answering. ■ I'm sorry but you did say that.
■ Don't worry, nobody reads the headlines/beyond the first paragraph/the captions/the back page. ■ Of course I checked the spelling.

THE OFFICIAL LIARS' HANDBOOK

Kids

■ Nobody wears/does/has it/them. ■ Everybody wears/does/has it/them. ■ I don't know but it wasn't me. ■ I always have to do it. ■ I never get to do it. ■ It's not my turn. ■ I'll do it later. ■ I did it earlier. ■ I won't do it again. ■ It's only a cough drop. ■ I was sick. ■ I don't remember that. ■ Nobody told me. ■ My little brother put it in the washing machine. ■ I left it at home/school. ■ My little sister drew on it. ■ Mom said I didn't have to. ■ She hit me first. ■ I'm full. ■ I don't need to blow my nose. ■ I cleaned my room. ■ I'll clean my teeth during the next commercial.

The Law

■ I'll need a few thousand to pay off the police/judge. ■ The judge reneged on the deal. ■ This won't take long, Your Honor. ■ I ask you, ladies and gentlemen, would a police officer jeopardize his career by lying under oath? ■ My client has no intention of leaving the country and looks forward to the opportunity of clearing his name. ■ I am instructed that . . . ■ My learned friend . . . ■ I am indebted to Your Honor for pointing out to me the fallacy of my argument. ■ Mr. X has put the case for the defendant with great vigor, clarity and persuasiveness, however . . . ■ I specialize in real estate/criminal law/business law. ■ If I am running a little bit late, don't worry, I will have contacted the court. ■ I have got you an excellent lawyer who is much older than he looks. ■ You don't pay a cent if we lose; but I must have cash up front. ■ Don't worry, I will consent to an adjournment. ■ This is my final offer. ■ I'd offer more if it was my decision, but the claims manager is very tough. ■ I only accept cash because checks take too long to clear. ■ We'll reserve it on appeal.

THE OFFICIAL · LIARS' HANDBOOK

Local Government

■ Your letter is being actively considered. ■ Your letter is being considered. ■ Your letter will be considered at the next meeting of the subcommittee. ■ The officer dealing with your letter is on leave. ■ Of course we are concerned about your problem. ■ I've got the numbers to get it through council. ■ The Democrats stopped it from going through. ■ The Republicans stopped it from going through. ■ The Bureaucrats stopped it from going through. ■ I've never taken a bribe. ■ The Town Planner's a friend of mine. ■ The Town Planner knows the score. ■ The Health Inspector's a friend of mine. ■ The Health Inspector knows the score. ■ You'll like the new zoning, just trust me. ■ I don't care what the Governor wants; we run this council. ■ I am not using my position in local government as a stepping-stone to national politics. ▓ The Governor's a friend of mine. ▓ I don't have anything to gain personally from this decision. ▓ I have absolute faith in the Mayor. ▓ The Mayor has my unequivocal support. ▓ I had absolutely no knowledge what my officers were doing.

Love

■ Everyone does this, it's perfectly natural. ■ It's dangerous to your health to get excited and then stop. ■ I'll stop as soon as you say. ■ That was great. ■ It gets better after you've done it a few times. ■ Nobody can hear us. ■ I'm not that kind of person. ■ I'm waiting for someone. ■ That's all over. ■ We have an open relationship. ■ I wish I'd met you before I met her. ■ I'll tell her tonight. ■ I couldn't tell her last night because we had visitors. ■ I couldn't tell her last night because she'd had a hard day. ■ The clinic said I was clear. ■ Size doesn't matter. ■ I've never felt this way before. ■ I'll call you. ■ Sorry, I don't have the phone on. ■ You knew I was married when we met — why is it different now? ■ I thought you understood my situation.

■ What's the rush? — we've got the rest of our lives.
■ It was only a physical thing. ■ It has made
our marriage stronger. ■ You'll get over
him/her. ■ I'll never put myself
through this again.

Meetings

■ No one will notice if you leave early. ■ You can use my parking spot. ■ You can sit at the back. ■ You only have to make an appearance. ■ Nothing can go wrong. ■ You won't have to stand again. ■ I'll try to get there. ■ We're all in this together. ■ The meeting starts at 7.30. ■ We'll be right behind you. ■ Supper is included. ■ You won't have to say anything. ■ I've spoken to them — they won't give you any trouble. ■ No one can tell if you're lying. ■ The room is air conditioned. ■ There won't be any violence. ■ Nobody is going to ask you that. ■ Childcare available. ■ Nobody will recognize you. ■ You'll be home by 10.

Men

■ I've been working long hours lately.
■ It's not your fault. ■ I've had too much to drink. ■ The bed creaks.
■ I can't think above the traffic noise.
■ It's too early. ■ It's too late.
■ I've eaten too much. ■ A good sleep will fix it. ■ If only you hadn't said what you said a minute ago.
■ We've had too much fun to spoil it.
■ Sex isn't everything. ■ This has nothing to do with my mother.

■ I've been having a lot of pain down there lately. ■ I read an article today.
■ I'm allergic to rubber. ■ You talked too much over dinner. ■ You didn't talk to me coming home. ■ We'll try again when we wake up.
■ I can hear the phone ringing. ■ I don't think I turned off the heater.
■ I just want to read tonight. ■ You really are sexy. ■ I can't help it.
■ I have no influence over it. ■ It has a mind of its own. ■ This has never happened before.

Model Making

■ This part fits here. ■ Only gentle pressure is needed. ■ It won't break if held right. ■ All pieces are intact and in the box. ■ The directions are in English/simple to follow/not necessary. ■ This is an authentic figure of the Napoleonic era. ■ I don't play with my models, they are works of art. ■ An easy snap-together kit. ■ I made it from scratch. ■ Don't worry, paint fixes gaps/glue globs/broken bits. ■ It's supposed to look war damaged.

Nursing

■ This won't hurt. ■ This won't take long. ■ I'll be back in a minute. ■ He's a very reputable surgeon. ■ This is the normal procedure. ■ The doctor wouldn't operate unless she/he thought it was absolutely necessary. ■ It's normal to have a certain amount of pain after this procedure. ■ Complications after this operation are rare. ■ You can go home in the morning. ■ The doctor will be in to see you tomorrow. ■ We won't shave too much off for the operation. ■ It's nothing to worry about. ■ The side effects are minimal. ■ The doctor won't keep you waiting much longer. ■ Hospital food isn't as bad as they say. ■ He/she died peacefully. ■ You'll be up and about in no time.

Officials

■ You've just missed him. ■ He should be back by three o'clock.
■ I'll get him to call as soon as he comes in. ■ There is no one in
that department at the moment. He's on the phone, will you wait?
■ I'll just put you through — click, beepbeepbeep. . . ■ We
have no one here by that name. ■ No, it wasn't me you were
talking to last week. ■ I'm afraid I don't work in this section
— I just answered the phone. ■ Thank you for your letter.
■ Your claim is being processed. ■ I apologise for the delay in responding
to your letter. ■ We can't find your file at the moment. ■ I have your file
in front of me, but I don't see any reference to that. ■ We never received
your form. ■ Don't worry about that letter unless you get another one.

Parents

■ At your age I was up every morning at six o'clock. ■ You'll thank me for this one day. ■ I don't expect gratitude. ■ She/he tells me everything. ■ You know what they're up to when they're at home. ■ We've never had that problem. ■ We don't care what he wants to be as long as he's happy. ■ The thing is to show you trust them. ■ It's not her, it's her friends. ■ It's just a phase. ■ You'll understand when you're older. ■ Actually I've come to enjoy that music. ■ There was a funny streak in her father's/mother's family. ■ Luckily she still prefers horses. ■ They're upstairs listening to records. ■ I'll tell her you rang. ■ We were pretty wild at that age. ■ Well at least he isn't gay.

Parties

- I'm not going to drink much tonight.
- They'll all be wearing jeans.
- They won't be here before seven at least.
- No one will want beer.
- That's sure to be enough pasta.
- What a lovely house.
- That's a nice wine.
- Red wine stains come out easily with soda water/salt.
- It wasn't one of our best glasses.
- There are no bones in this fish.
- I made the pâté myself.
- It's just a mild curry.
- The neighbours are very tolerant.

■ Just half a glass, thanks. ■ He doesn't normally act like this when he's been drinking. ■ I've really enjoyed talking to you. ■ I'm not tired at all. ■ It was a lovely party. ■ Your friends are such interesting people. ■ It's no trouble to give you a lift home. ■ It's no trouble if you stay the night.

The Personnel Office

▓   Your vacation money will be ready before you leave.   ▓   We'll correct it next pay period—it won't happen again.   ▓   Sorry, we had already processed the check, but it will be taken care of next pay period.   ▓   I'm sorry, the computer is down.   ▓   Your check will be ready after 12:30 P.M.   ▓   The check will be ready after 3 P.M.   ▓   We'll have a check ready in the morning.   ▓   We'll call you when the check's ready.   ▓   Nobody told us you'd been given a raise.

Political Press Secretaries

■ Don't quote me, but it's fair to say . . . ■ I will call you back. ■ That does not come within this department. ■ Ring Mr X in the Department—he can help. ■ No, I haven't mentioned it to anyone else. ■ I can help you tomorrow/next week. ■ He/she has the numbers. ■ This is the first I've heard of it. ■ The report isn't finished yet. ■ It's being considered. ■ She's quite a find. ■ That was out of context. ■ That's an internal matter. ■ It was an independent selection committee. ■ He was not drunk. ■ He ran into a door. ■ He/she is at a meeting. ■ I've been trying to get you all afternoon.

■ It's a fact-finding/study tour.

■ He's looking forward to his
new appointment. ■ We don't pay
attention to opinion polls.

■ He's on the road traveling and
I can't reach him.

Publishing

■ I've got your manuscript on the top of the pile. ■ We'll have it out in plenty of time for Christmas. ■ It's a standard contract. ■ Nobody's ever asked to change that clause before. ■ The editor won't change anything significant. ■ We've found a terrific illustrator. ■ We'll pick up that mistake in the galleys. ■ We'll pick up that mistake in the reprint. ■ Nobody will notice that mistake anyway. ■ The publisher will look after all libel and copyright problems. ■ We never pay a bigger advance than that. ■ We're working on a joint publication overseas. ■ We can do a reprint in two weeks if necessary. ■ You'll have plenty of time to correct the proofs. ■ We always pay royalties on the due date. ■ The jacket design is terrific. ■ Of course we've spelled your name correctly.

■ We'll give you a big launching party. ■ It doesn't matter that it wasn't reviewed/mentioned on radio/mentioned on TV. ■ Reviews/radio/TV don't sell books anyway.

Radio Interviewing

■ Yes, I've read your book. ■ I enjoyed your book. ■ This'll only take a few minutes. ■ That was great, just what we wanted. ■ We'll just have to edit out a few bits, mostly mine, ha. ha. ■ Can we call you again if we want more on the subject of the articulated moth wing? ■ We're sending one of our most senior reporters. ■ Thank you for your time, Your Honor. ■ We can't supply copies of tapes. ■ The tape was accidentally erased. ■ We'll play this tomorrow for sure. ■ It's not my fault, the producer edited it out.

Restaurants

■ Good evening, nice to see you again.
■ We just had a cancellation. ■ That is a full portion, sir. ■ I'm terribly sorry. ■ All our dishes are home made. ■ If you have any complaints, the chef will be only too happy to hear about them. ■ We've never had any complaints about this before. ■ The fish is flown in fresh every day. ■ It looks like a real dive from the outside but the food's great.
■ Anyway, it's not the food but the atmosphere that's important. ■ Anyway, it's not the atmosphere but the food that's important.

■ Oh, yes, we have a note of your booking. ■ We have a very nice house wine. ■ Half the fun of eating Chinese is using the chopsticks. ■ That's the first cockroach/mouse/worm/piece of glass we've ever had in our food. ■ The ..... (any slow-moving dish) is very popular.

Sales Assistants

■ Unbelievably low prices. ■ You'll never have another opportunity like this. ■ It's the last one in stock. ■ A never-to-be-repeated offer. ■ Take it on time payment — it won't cost you a thing. ■ Below cost. ■ Precision-made by a craftsman. ■ You'll have no trouble with it. ■ That colour suits you. ■ They'll stretch after a while. ■ It won't shrink. ■ That's the length everyone is wearing now. ■ It's much warmer than it looks. ■ No one will notice that. ■ It's uncrushable. ■ It's the last one in the shop.

■ Bring it back if you don't like it.   ■ We can deliver next week.   ■ You can have any colour you like.   ■ This sort of thing never goes out of fashion. ■ You won't see this anywhere else.

THE OFFICIAL · LIARS HANDBOOK

Teachers

■ They're a great bunch of kids, really. ■ It's only a tiny minority who'll give you trouble. ■ I know I can trust you to take this money to the office. ■ Go on, I'm listening. ■ He's a great principal—he's been into equal opportunity for years. ■ The staff here are very ethical/professional/ hardworking/friendly/helpful. ■ There's plenty of paper. ■ None of the parents could possibly object to this novel/film/play/syllabus/course/ excursion. ■ This experiment is completely harmless. ■ I work a 48-hour week as it is. ■ I'll mark these tonight. ■ I'm always available to talk to parents. ■ We encourage parents to be involved in their children's education. ■ I'd worry about them if they were too quiet. ■ The next person who talks will go outside.

■ Thanks, class, for the gorgeous china dog. ■ Of course I'll be at the game. ■ Even the first graders behave better than that.

■ You'll stay in at lunchtime. ■ I'm not going to tell you again. ■ Our staff meetings are brief but extremely useful. ■ You'll love this novel — it's extremely relevant to your lifestyles. ■ I'm not doing this for my own sadistic pleasure, you know. ■ I just loved working with you all.

THE OFFICIAL · LIARS' HANDBOOK

The Theatre

■ You were great — it's just the balance of the cast. ■ The critics were smiling when they left the theatre. ■ The gun will go off. ■ Once you're in costume the lines will make more sense. ■ Under the lights you'll lose 10 years. ■ Under the lights you'll gain 10 years. ■ This was a major hit at last year's Playwrights' Conference. ■ You would have been great for a play I directed last year.

■ The author wants to sit in on rehearsal, and won't say a word. ■ The dressing rooms have a shower and toilet. ■ The dressing room has a toilet. ■ We'll get a bucket backstage. ■ He doesn't stutter once he's on stage. ■ The chickens are trained — they'll stay in the cage. ■ The songs will be written in plenty of time for the opening. ■ We're using a real needle but I won't actually stick it in your arm. ■ We're cutting some of your lines but it's nothing to do with your performance. ■ Of course you don't look silly.

Train Travel

■ It should be here any minute now. ■ It's only a couple of minutes late. ■ Train journeys take the worry out of travelling. ■ We apologise for any inconvenience. ■ The train has been cancelled due to technical difficulties. ■ Our timetables have been drawn up by surveying passenger needs. ■ The train on platform four goes to . . . ■ Our new seats are vandal-proof. ■ We have the backing of the travelling public in this dispute. ■ Our men are striking for a principle. ■ This train has been cancelled for today only. ■ The next one will be less crowded.

NEXT TRAIN

Universities

■ Teaching is the most important part of our job. ■ I'll have your essays marked by next week. ■ That's an interesting comment. ■ You won't lose marks if you disagree with me. ■ You're welcome to come and see me to discuss your work. ■ That's an original piece of research. ■ We respect students' opinions. ■ You'll find this course interesting/stimulating/rewarding/socially relevant. ■ There's not much written work.
■ There are copies available in the university bookshop. ■ I'm not just arguing for the sake of arguing. ■ You should be able to recognise all the organs from the diagram in the text. ■ I welcome criticism.
■ I've almost finished the thesis. ■ I do my best work at home.
■ This department is run democratically. ■ We regard secretaries/

typists/clerical staff/gardeners as important members of the university.
■   I'll spend most of my sabbatical in libraries.   ■   I envy your working
with your hands.   ■   There won't be anything in the exam that's unfamiliar
to you.   ■   (d) all of the above.   ■   (e) none of the above.

Your 30th Birthday

■ It's not how old you are, it's how old you feel. ■ You don't look it.
■ This will be the year it all really happens for you. ■ The stars are in your favor. ■ It's a lucky number. ■ I'll get you your real present soon.
■ We'll go out and celebrate. ■ It's the thought that counts. ■ It's a beautiful age. ■ Women look their best after 30. ■ Men over 30 can attract women of any age. ■ Lots of people do their best work later in life. ■ The worst 30 years of your life are over. ■ Such a relief not to have the insecurities of the immature. ■ You have the body of a 28-year-old. ■ Youth is wasted on the young. ■ Everything gets better as you get older. ■ Birthdays aren't important. ■ You only need to worry when you turn 40.

Acknowledgements

Many of these great lies originally appeared in the "Stay In Touch" column of *The Sydney Morning Herald*, and we must acknowledge the creative efforts of the readers of that column. These are but a few of the contributors: for Advertising Agencies, Noel Adams; for Babies, Jeremy Pragnell, Helen Fulton and Georgina Gentle; for the Building Trade, Jack Tarlington; for Car Repair, Stephen Ramshaw and Tony Melville; for Childbirth, Allan Cala and Georgina Gentle; for Computers, Peter Martin, Howard Harrison, and Francis Young; for Delicatessens, Alison Shaw; for Dieting, Jessie Bartos; for Drivers, H. Jeffery; for Hairdressing, Leticia Grant; for Home Dressmaking, Carmen Cadzow; for Home Handymen, Mike Hennessey; for International Travel, S. and A. Jeans and Yolanda Latif; for Journalism, Tracey Aubin and many others; for Kids, Alex

Robinson, Ruth Ellison; for Local Government, Tony Reeves and Jeanie Ivanins; for Love, Leticia Grant, Belinda Hamilton, B. H. Cohen, and Nathalie Brown; for Meetings, Anthony English; for Men, Helen Russell; for Model Making, Tony Grummels; for Nursing, Alaric Giles and Judy Mather; for Officials, Sam Friend and Trapper Tom; for Parents, J. Holt; for Parties, Barbara Troy; for the Personnel Office, Ruth Livingstone; for Publishing, T. Johns and Jacqueline Kent; for Restaurants, Joe Perrone; for Sales Assistants, David Gordon, C. Perrott, and Graham Jenkins; for Teachers, Roger Knox, Ruth Ellison, Schira Cleary, David and Megan Llewellyn, and Catherine Williams; for Theatre, Katherine Thomson; for Train Travel, David Gordon, Paul Mattes; for Universities, Megan and David Llewellyn, and Jenny O'Neill; for Your 30th Birthday, Inez Baranay.